E{M}MA+

the ghost orchids

Published simultaneously in the United States and
Great Britain in 2017 by Pretend Genius
Copyright © Sean Brijbasi

ISBN: 978-0-9852133-8-1

"I write this not for the many, but for you, each of us is enough of an audience for the other."

—*Seneca*

for e{m}ma+

for always

matter

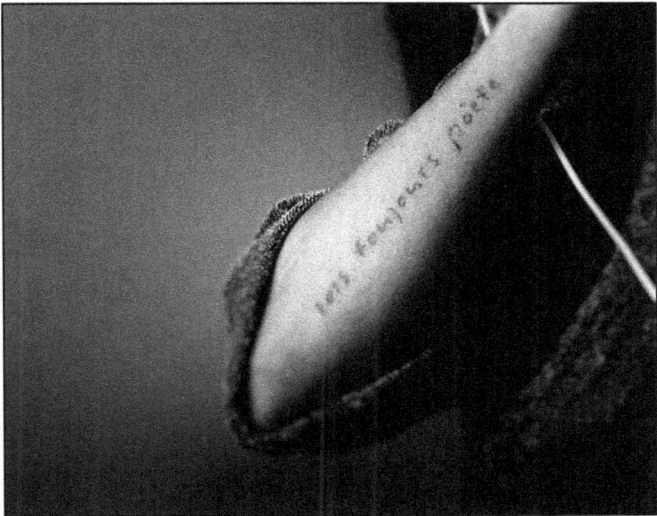

I think
her name
was ~~Alice~~
     Felice

part 1 – mumble mumble   △

1

I pass by the house every week on my way home. Light comes from behind the tall trees in the front yard that block the wooden facade. At dusk, in a certain shade, this house reminds me of you. On other days it is someone else's house and I drive by without noticing. But on these days I think that in another life we are living there together, that I am calling to you from the bedroom upstairs while you walk to the mailbox (you can't hear me but this is a different type of not-hearing). In the other life something makes you stay. I know. But I also don't know. In this life you are not with me and I drive past the house and continue on my way home.

2

Dear you, an altogether faithful friend who is not me,

I think that in this life you also have moments when you sense that we are together in another life. Maybe when you are about to fall asleep and feel that I am there beside you. When you have your window opened and a breeze blows into the room and over your face at a certain angle on a certain type of morning. But only at that time and no other. Only at that time and then the feeling passes and you continue with your day unencumbered by the feeling. At other times maybe you think about someone else. Maybe you leave your window open at night when you fall asleep.

--S.

3

I don't send the letter. I lay it on the small table by the door. I don't have an envelope. So many words I have written and no way to transmit them. I lie down on the couch and let the feeling of what is happening around me come over me. I almost feel it. I make tea in a small, white cup and drink it while I stare through the window. I sip until darkness and wait for something to happen. But nothing happens. I write a darkness song. I have the melody in my head. I have the words in my head. They just come to me like music.

4

Complete darkness in the morning
Complete darkness in the day

Complete darkness in the sunshine
Complete darkness in the rain

Complete darkness when you're on holiday
Complete darkness when you stay

Complete darkness
Complete darkness
Complete darkness

It's dark in here

Good memories have become vague. Good memories have become bad. Good memories disappearing appear to make me sad.

They come from the city. The city that is yours and that is also mine. To say that I was born here is to say that wherever you were born that you were also born here. The apartment that is yours and that is also mine. The way I see the dust and the way you see the dust that travels by sunlight and steals through the apartment window after we have returned from a long night of drink and philosophy, the exudation of which makes us crave the opium den of another time, where we can escape our sometimes wearying instinct to resist and instead gaze at the silhouettes of paper birds flying against the backdrop of a white sheet to let ourselves be weak for a little while.

What is all of this if not madness? The madness that the world which I was brought into can turn against me and (worse) turn myself against me—that its feeble arguments might be enough to make me a collaborator against myself—that it could make me think that it was never good enough to be just me.

But we have met in this same life and something inside is telling me to reach out to you. I will convince you and bring you to my apartment home. The cloud only feet from the ground where prophets protest below us. They want to take our dreams from us. We can't let them. We'll take the bicycle short-cut to the aluminum shop then pedal back at different speeds (because the songs in our heads are different).

You:

To the coast
We'll be masking our
Own way
Yeah

Me:

I know this fight
I'm that personage
In the air

Freedom

6

I was born in Skeldon, Berbice. My father was a
spice trader. My mother was a singer. I spent my
early years travelling with my father (as far that
way as Mongolia and as far that way as Lapland).
He taught me how to be human. In my teens I
played the banjo and served as a back-up singer for
my mother's all-beautiful band. She taught me how
to be human. At the age of seventeen, I left home
on a ship bound for the new world. I was fluent in

English although my cosmopolitan municipal was uncertain of my fluency. But there was evidence in my letters to suggest that I had a well-grounded understanding of the language. The ship (christened "HMS Sinkerton") sank off the coast of the continent. All of its passengers except for me drowned.

The waves roughed me up but I braced myself against the roughness and surfed to shore on a piece of wood from the sinking ship. I surfed for six days. On the seventh day when I reached the shore I threw the piece of wood onto the sand and saw the word "Sin" written underneath. I took it as a sign, dropped to my knees, and renounced all of my material possessions (a blouse, eight coins, a boot, a hat, three pencils, and a pair of dice).

7

I made the darkness song more cosmopolitan. From the provincial I took the fears. I added lyrics. It sounds good. In my head sounds sound super. I'm thinking of sounding everything there.

Complete darkness when you're smiling
Complete darkness when you're in tears

Complete darkness when you're on top of it
Complete darkness when you're falling away

Complete darkness when you're dreaming
Complete darkness when you're awake

Complete darkness
Complete darkness
Complete darkness

It's dark in here

8

I read that some philosophical people can't listen to the repetitive sounds of modern music because it reminds them of the inevitable ending of life. The ever-going pounding of the heart until the abrupt or faded ending of the song (as in life). I pretend to avoid such rhythms even though I secretly yearn for them because the ever-going pounding of the heart is for the young and curious.

9

~~I wish I still had my hat. I thought that triumph followed renouncement. The hat was a gift from X. She took photographs of me wearing her hat. I asked her if I could have it. She said no but she bought me the same hat for my birthday.~~

~~I didn't think that renouncing my hat meant renouncing X. I just don't see her or talk to her anymore. I thought the hat would lead to bigger things but it didn't. I didn't have a crisis renouncing the hat. I came to think of it as a goodbye present. The only thing I want to renounce now is my renouncement. But I can't see myself falling to my knees anymore. Even for that.~~

~~Renouncement is a distinct feeling and I don't want to feel distinct feelings anymore. I want them to all merge into one. Something with all tempos, colors, flavors, and wind speeds.~~

We are going to make it you and I even if
you're not thinking about making it and go this way
or that way with anyone who interests you.
Because you are by yourself and I am by myself.

I should have finished the letter. I could have
purchased an envelope or even made one out of
other pieces of paper. Not finishing is a flimsy
excuse for being incomplete.

10

On the simple chance that I lose my way when I
am riding I follow her. Her bicycle is stable. I
think I would like to ride beside her instead of
behind her but I don't know the song in her head. I
could guess. But if I guess wrong then I might fall
further behind. And what if I speed ahead of her
instead? Then I would get lost and she might
disappear behind me. If I start humming then the
song in her head would gradually change to the
song in my head and I think we would be riding
next to each other. But if her song suddenly
stopped because I intruded and all the music in her

head was gone (if she crashes) then I would crash too. Maybe I wouldn't crash but I would crash on purpose so she wouldn't feel bad. And what if the change was like two tennis players exchanging sides of a tennis court? Then we would have exchanged songs and again I would be lost.

11

We're not going to the country. We're going to the city. And to a very particular place in the city. Riding high. This is city. Riding high and fast. City strutting.

She turns to me and I worry she's not looking at where she's going. I think that she must be careful. It's getting dark and she's pedalling super-fast. Hey beautiful girl. Slow down. I'm just gazing at her and don't see the curb-side which I hit with the front wheel of my bicycle.

She stops and bends over with her hair and her face and her entire body and lifts my bicycle upright. I look up and see an apartment window with a light on and someone looking at me. I stand up and we walk our bicycles to Le Carillon. Our arms touch and I walk in such a way as to continue this touching.

I want a coffee in the bar but everyone is drinking a beer. I order a tea but they don't have tea. I have a beer and so do you. Where is the nuance of life in a place like this? I don't see it. I sometimes think you're not so interested in me but maybe your nuance is difficult to detect.

H. is there. He calls over to you. I know he sees me. But he calls you anyway. And you go, telling me you'll return soon. But soon turns into something that is not soon. And now I have to pretend. I have to hide my shame. So in my head I think of my darkness song. I want to add to it but nothing's coming to me. Nothing's coming to me because I'm watching you laughing with H. I go outside to smoke. Smoking has saved me from many bad situations. I just say I'll be back. But I go outside where you can't see me and I watch you through the window.

When I think of *genuine euphoria* I think of igniting the soul. A localized geographical fire of the cilia of the human passions. In the other life we are more slender and mammalian. We meet ignited. Fire in search of fire. But I think we must be looking for more than that.

There is in this life only the struggle of overcoming the obstacles, which we ourselves and others, have placed before us.

I know of H.'s whereabouts. He has a pretty girlfriend he plays tennis with. I've seen them at the tennis court. They look like they are higher on the scale of happiness than I am. But I am not after happiness. When I see it I just think that instead of chasing other feelings I could chase happiness. But I have grown accustomed to the feeling of the mild unpleasantness of life, which is the most someone of my dark-songed nature could ever hope for.

H. is making elaborate plans for my destruction but he will fail because a simple plan will do.

14

At my apartment the fire alarm rings and a voice comes through a speaker telling everyone to leave the building. So I do. I take the stairs with everyone else. I wait outside with everyone else. I look up at the building for smoke. Many people talk with their hands in their pockets because it is cold.

I'm thinking about you when the voice comes from somewhere behind or on top of the building and tells everyone that we may go back inside.

The voice. The way it comes through the air. The interruption of my thoughts. The crowd.

I pick up a rock and throw it through a second floor window. The sound of the glass breaking flares me up.

"Revolution!" I yell at the building. "Fuck you pigs!"

And then I walk like a sheep with the other sheep towards the building. But I stop. I don't go inside. Even though I'm shivering from cold I stay outside for another hour. This is the form of my resistance to power. I do harm to myself. I go back inside when I think that no one could mistake me for obeying. I make tea, wrap my body in a blanket, and look through the broken glass. I see the rock underneath my table. I can't tell if what I'm feeling is shame but I think it's very close.

fuck you pigs !

15

I will spill me up far into so many corridors and nooks and become thinner as I flood into the creases that are the peninsulas of the human soul.

In this life you live far away. Maybe as far away as around the world. I remember having lunch with someone from America and then later that evening wandering into a tent pitched by other tents behind a house where no one lived. This could be the house of our meeting. If I let curiosity and courage escort me—each taking one hand—but I become distracted. There are noises coming from other tents. People conducting manoeuvres in the fields and I am overcome (in that small moment) by a feeling most closely resembling happiness.

16

Wherever she goes she makes the space more beautiful. She's going everywhere so everywhere is becoming more beautiful. What else is there to do in this world but to take your body to different places and make those places more beautiful? Sometimes I see her dance with her red lipstick and twirl around with her dress and legs and arms and hair. Sometimes the place is even more beautiful after she leaves because she becomes missing. I look at the empty spaces she leaves behind and sometimes walk through them when I think no one is watching.

17

A few nights ago I tiptoed into H's apartment with a saw and cut his arm off. His forehand is more erratic now but his volley has improved. He still has a superb backhand.

And yet you talk about him more than ever even though there is less of him to talk about. In the minds of some people you are acting incomprehensibly.

There was no reason to disarm H. but he doesn't seem bothered. He flips the tennis ball into the air with his racquet and then hits his serve (all with the same arm), which still has the same power and spin as always. I think that you are probably more impressed than ever. I don't think H. notices that his arm is missing. He hasn't said anything to me and shakes my hand after our matches as always. I smile at him now even when I lose.

I don't understand how anyone could love H. He's not me. I don't get the sense that he understands the entire universe. But he has a great forehand. He uses two hands, which is unusual. He generates a lot of pace.

If I think of the tennis ball as the world, he just beats it around. He doesn't shape it. He batters it. I think about H.'s girlfriend. I like her (even though she likes H.) but I don't understand why she doesn't like me more than she likes H. I understand but it doesn't make sense to me. It's senseless.

He's not letting her win any points. And she just claps for him and smiles. What's she going to do next? Wipe his neck with a towel? H. is a demon. H. is destroying the world.

When someone destroys the world he destroys it indiscriminately even if he has a destruction purpose in mind—like a car crash performing surgery—so that both the ugly and the beautiful are destroyed.

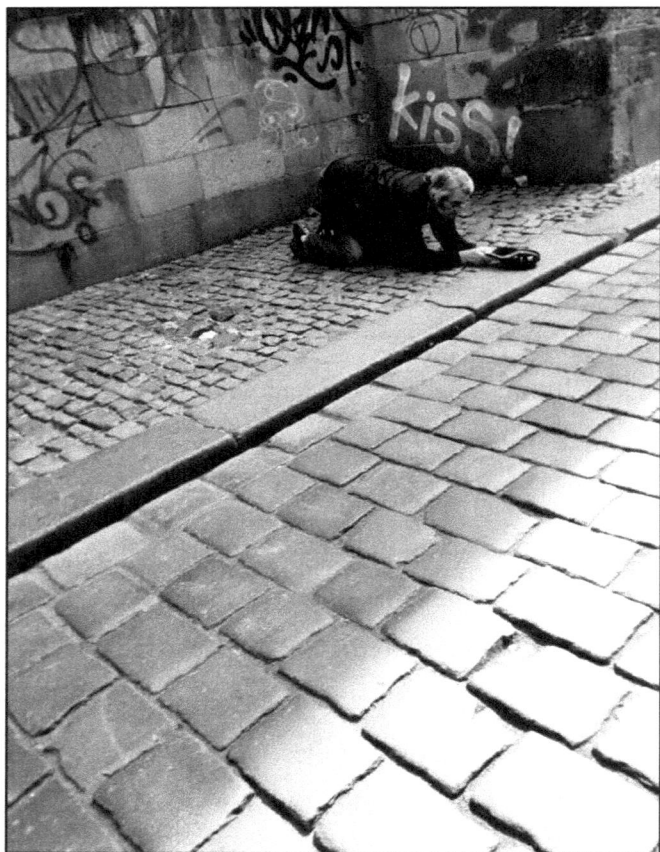

1

How is it possible that the death of someone I never spoke to and had seen only a handful of times could affect me in such a way?

Was it just the right time in my life to be affected? Was it because she represented something that I wasn't aware of? Had she become a part of the fabric of my life (somewhere on the frayed edges) that I didn't notice?

And then there was the man who dressed up as a dolphin and rode his bicycle around the city. He was killed by a falling sheet of glass on Gustav Adolfsgatan a few weeks after the girl died. Of all the people in the city. The man who dressed up as a dolphin.

I know there is a mathematical equation that connects the death of these two people. I know that this mathematical equation is more consequential than anything currently explaining the universe.

2

In this life we are together but in another life I am driving past the house you live in with someone else. In this life we are happy. We have children.

But I have memories of seeing a girl in the window of a building. I crash on my bicycle and look up to see if anyone is watching. Our eyes meet.

I feel like I know this girl. But I don't quite remember. I was only a child. But what are these vague memories from childhood, these orphans, that won't leave me? I can't put them into context. I can't connect them to the present.

3

We're getting ready for the masquerade party. I have my masque and you have your masque. We're hanging fabric from the ceiling. I'm holding the ladder for you. I look up every now and then. I think about people driving or walking by our house. You're high up. Sometimes I hear you walking up and down the stairs.

Who do I think is there? Will you be someone else when you open the door? The ceiling fan spins. Could it all disappear or become something else? The fabric slips from your hand and drops to the floor. I would have to pretend that I recognize you or whoever you are might think something is wrong with me. It would take me a few hours or even a few days to piece it all together but you wouldn't notice and life would go on as usual. I would still love you.

4

Where to start on my equation?

(I will start with numbers.)

But I know there are always letters in equations.

(I can think about it. Just keep thinking about it and it will come to me.)

I didn't go to the archery range today. I like shooting at circles. Circles are sometimes part of an equation. Circles also have their own equation.

You and I have a circle. I try to make an Aristotelian something of our circle instead of just letting the circle exist. Sometimes I feel that you're starting to leave our circle. I try to understand this leaving and why I can't make an Aristotelian something of our circle to keep you from leaving. And then—*E{M}*

I think there are three areas of something new that my equation will introduce to the world. It will be a new world with the untangled bodies of the human species and their limbs accursed of convergence. Or perhaps the opposite.

You look at me while you lick the flap of an envelope. You've put a letter in it. I hope it's not my equation you've put in there. Beautiful woman.

5

Sometimes I think of you and you are mine and sometimes I think of you and you are not mine. Because sometimes you are mine and sometimes you are not mine. Sometimes when you are mine I think you are not mine. And sometimes when you are not mine I think you are mine.

I came to your window with a bouquet of flowers in hand and called to you from below. I couldn't get past the gate in the front yard. Your window was open but you didn't answer. I thought I saw the light on in your apartment (the glow of the streetlamp confused me). But your absence couldn't convince me of your absence and I threw a flower toward the opening while I called your name. The flower hit the ledge beneath the window and fell into the yard below. The sudden and unexpected crash surprised me.

I wish I knew the names of flowers. I could catalogue them and document the consequences of their flight for posterity.

The second flower hit the bottom of the window pane and spun into the room. It took damage during its ingress and I imagined it lying wounded on the floor for you to find.

I thought you could read my mind. Wherever you were why couldn't you read it then? I was there waiting for you. I know this city.

The third flower—the last flower because I had resolved to find my aim—struck the glass and left a mark before it dropped onto the ledge and lay there.

A sudden rage (my rages are sudden) overcame me and I flung the remaining bouquet toward the building hoping to raze it to the ground in a tumult of destruction. But the flowers separated in the air and landed on the grass without a sound.

I know this city. I know the ways of the alleys and boulevards that lead to other places. And along the way both the glistening and powdery-filmed lives of the people who live and work on them.

You could have followed me. You could have followed me with your heart and I would have shown you the secret passageways to a revolution.

6

I have questions but the world is quiet. Always quiet. Knowing everything but giving nothing. Even when we are alone and I make unspeakable promises to keep its secrets (my promises are always unspeakable). Still nothing. So I will ask you and you and you.

But know that when I ask you I am asking the world. It is from the world that I want to know and if your answers seem not of this world then I will ask another until I am sated.

But are you not of this world? Are you not grounded in the salt and loam of the moor? Does your hand not touch the grain still connected to the stalks and shoots that pox the earth's surface? I too will be asked and I will answer. I too am of the world.

I read your letter and sense that you are being transformed by your undertaking while I remain the same. I also wish to be transformed but sense that a part of me will not allow it.

Dear S.,

I wait for the rain and our chance to walk together underneath your expansive parapluie. I look for it from my window. I wait. I know that when it rains I will see it and know that you are beneath it.

E.

7

I call to you through your window. I move my expansive parapluie to my shoulder so I can see you. My favourite object in the world is my expansive parapluie, though it wasn't my favourite until you walked beneath it.

You come downstairs and we walk toward the park. There is a bench beneath a tree that stays dry if the wind is calm (we sit on the bench, alone in the park, under my expansive parapluie and the summer rain). But today we keep walking. Through the park, past our bench, to the other side where the row of trees end, toward Le Carillon, hearing the rain and the machines and the murmur of the living.

And in this rain, in the turmoil of this world, our souls are quietly set afire. I feel it in my chest and through my chest I feel it in yours.

A man walks past us and then calls from behind to ask about the time. But I know he doesn't care about the time. He only wants you to turn around so he can see your face again.

8

What is this equation that is tormenting me? It torments me when I am awake and when I am sleeping. If I could solve it in my sleep I could save my waking hours for you. But this equation is pressing down on me.

I want all the letters of my equation flowing in the same direction or even different directions and then something in a plane above or below.

You're cute when you're sleeping tight. I'm into you. And how.

If you fall asleep I would like to fall asleep also. If I am walking somewhere I would like to suddenly fall asleep when you fall asleep. If I am riding my bicycle through the park to Le Carillon then I would like to suddenly fall asleep when you fall asleep. Other humans will find me and take care of me until you wake up.

In other worlds everything is allowed and nothing has meaning. In other worlds nothing is allowed and everything has meaning. But in our world everything is allowed and everything has meaning.

I look around. I listen carefully to what people are saying ("it's blind in here", "women bring order to the universe"). I hear all the whispers and mumbling. Mumble mumble. Mumble mumble. I see people moving through space and watch the motionless objects they move around. The penny. The post box. The dead tree.

One day I will stop and knock on the door of a house and meet the people who live there. I will explain to them that I live in this house also and that

I've made changes to the library and started a small garden in the backyard. I sleep in the room below their bedroom. On the street outside my window I can see E. when she was a teenager lean her bicycle against the tree and run into the house.

part everything

{} +

I see the faces of my mother and father when I was young and I see them as they are now.

I know you live in the city and look to its horizons as a world beyond the tumult of these roadways.

Your city is encircled by gravestones. Your good and dedicated citizens form its border.

I walk the perimeter with those like me, wielding the blood axe, dressed in the shimmering silver, blowing bubbles from the plastic rings excavated from the country paddocks.

Our violence gang—the Ghost Orchids—meet here but today there is only you and me. Your weapon is the empty flower vase.

You fold the t-shirt I've made for you (it has the word "GO" painted on it) and put it in your luxury bag. I hide my axe and open my expansive parapluie. We sit on the bench under the sprinkle of rain and watch the Ferris wheel and hear the people on it scream. I tell you that if I keep looking at the wheel I will get dizzy. I am dizzy. Our legs touch (I hope you notice).

Beyond and through the giant wheel we see a stage. The drummer suckles his snare and bass with phat beats. The guitar player strums a riff. The singer turns to the crowd and drops to her knees. The crowd cheers.

But I wonder where the sun is in all of this? I tap my leg with my hand. We are too far away to hear the nuance. Instead I play a song in my head—a darkness song—because even during the fleeting happiness of the world and its good and cheering inhabitants and you sitting next to me wearing a dress that makes all things under the sun possible I still hope to send my destruction waves outward. But you lean into my shoulder and whisper in my ear. You tell me that you are glad we met. I feel your hair on my neck, on my face, and think that you have saved me and saved the world.

10

part hope ☆ part hopeless

{47}

You call to me from your window but I don't hear you. I'm mapping the city fissures through which demons emerge. I follow the trail of dark notes intoned by their exodus.

I hope I can still come around even though I didn't stop when you called. I'm busy, you see.

I think about my arm without its hand. Is there any point in keeping it? Perhaps I will lose my balance if I don't have both.

I hear you whisper: as the hand goes, so goes the arm. I am one of the living and the living have words they live by—as the hand goes, so goes the arm.

In the taxi I talk and you look out the window. The driver spies us in the rear view mirror. You're not sitting close enough to me. She's probably wondering if she can move in between us with her rambler eyes that have marked all destinations in her memory. But there's no destination to mark between us. You slide the taxi window down and the incoming breeze disquiets your hair.

I think we can look happy in the sunshine, sitting on the grass, in a garden of flowers, being shy with each other, as if that were the moment before we no longer contained ourselves and all that came after and was missed by the camera could not be explained by any artificial or human eye.

In the taxi you're sitting on my soon-to-be-non-arm side. Oh, how I pass my days thinking of it—a slow decay that will one day end with incision.

At night we'll see a lighthouse from the garden but we'll sit in chairs and not on the grass because there are insects. We'll see a boat tilting in the roughed up briny and someone floating on a piece of wood, holding on for his or her dear life. Then we'll hold hands and run toward the sea never thinking that maybe it would have been better to cry out for help.

strikes! for justice

Our violence gang the Ghost Orchids have caused a stir in the city. We are ghosts to the people but orchids to ourselves. There are only two of us now but we still create mishap. We paint melons and bananas on the city buildings and leave books about cigars and oysters here and there. Sometimes I play a ukulele in the bushes. I once had feelings for these people but they are gone now. *They* equals *feelings* and *people*.

They come and go. I have no control of them. That's why I'm in a violence gang the likes of which the world has seen only a few times.

Our violence gang has several moves to hurt people very badly if we want to—most of the time for justice. We don't like to be in a group but there are only two of us now. And we have suffered.

Believe me we have suffered even if our suffering isn't linked to any biological needs. We feel guilty for the reasons that we suffer but we don't know why. We think our suffering is as painful as other suffering but maybe not as important.

With only two of us my thinking is clearer than before. I can think about math and science and draw interesting conclusions. With only two of us I can find equations to complex problems nine or ten times faster. For example, the death of two unrelated people. Some argue that people are related in some sense if only at the highest level (that we are all people—that we are all brothers and sisters in the same struggle). But my thinking is clearer and I tell you this isn't true.

"Do you want to go for a walk?" I ask.

"We're walking now", E. says.

"I know", I say. "But I mean a more formal walk. To the gardens and then about the gardens. We can sit on our bench and watch the giant Ferris wheel."

E. and I are sometimes-formalists. We use it as rebellion. I surprise her with a strike to her chest (the fist of strong) which she dodges (quick cat) before striking back with an elbow (the elbow of invincibility) to the top of my head. I am woozy but stay upright. I regain my focus on the foliage and flowers in the garden and settle into my gait. E. is a wonderful striker.

I think about the time she carried the heavy suitcase at the train station. I carried the light suitcase. Her breathing was heavy. My breathing was light. I talked as we walked while she was silent.

12

blasphemerry xmas balloons

I think about how to say good-bye. A hug, a smile, and a wave. Or a long embrace until your impending departure releases its grip from my chest. I'm practicing in my head (I'm panicking in my head).

I have crying-out memories of our window and our garden and our little room where we formed the tenets that make up our Ghost Orchid manifesto.

1. It is more fun to defy than to deny.
2. We defy what we should otherwise deny.
3. We acknowledge the existence of that we don't believe in because blasphemy is more fun than being silent unless being silent is blasphemous.

I think an embrace would be too much. I have only touched you a few times. I remember all of those times because they were so few. I think of them happening slowly. I remember the places on you that I touched. I think about the fabric through which my touching was transferred to your skin (I defied your fabric). I think about the time I touched the skin itself. With these hands and fingers. (I blasphemed against the purity of your skin). Perhaps with only a few fingers. But who could know in such moments?

Do you remember when the yellow and blue balloons came down from the room above ours, floating past our window? Imagine if I were on the other side of them. On the street looking up at you. I would barely see you through them until they all came down. But we move toward each other like ghosts. I would pass through them and be near you.

~~May I call you buttercup? Or bunch of wildflowers for the plucking? You tell me that I will be famous in the cast iron tub. But I don't take baths. Showers of powerful water is what I want descending on me—to wash away, once and for all, this slow decay that will one day keep us apart.~~

1

E. says that all that is bright in me shines only in dark places.

E. says that it is hard to keep something that belongs to no one else and that we have kept each other.

In the morning I will think about leaving and then leave but only to go from the bed to the love-seat in our room. I will think about painting and look at the picture of the woman with no eyes that E. pinned onto the wall with a pin she found between the crease of the floor and the wall. I will think about sculpting and look across the road at the pavement and the bending tree branches. I will think about making music and connect three or four notes in my head that I will later forget. I will think about taking photographs and look at the bowl of old apples and oranges on the table (only one orange by the time of this thinking) and imagine them in black and white. I will think about being graceful and walk across the room and then sit down at the small table by the window. I will sit completely still for several minutes and change the tone of the voice I hear in my head.

But this evening I hear the passage of E.'s bicycle on the sidewalk. I hear her feet as she alights. I hear the bicycle frame rattle the fence chain. I hear the creaks of the building's front door, her footsteps on the stairs (she's running). I hear the door of our small apartment open behind me and feel the breeze that travels in with her. Soon it will be dark.

E. and I grow in the dark. All of our flowering buds appear as if by magic at first light and then die before they bloom.

She takes an orange from the bowl and sits down at the table with me. She peels it and leaves the pieces of skin on the table. I arrange them into the shape of an arrow that points to the open window. She breaks the fruit apart and gives me half.

The sun is setting. E. and I eat our orange. She takes a small bite and wipes the juice from her lips. Chews. Swallows. Starts again.

6-6

part 2 - tennis is fun

We're talking about going somewhere and becoming stranded. Just the two of us. We're not saying it but everything we say makes it clear that we know what we're really talking about. Not clear to others. But clear to you and me. The more we talk the more our words create a new place for only us. We live in this new place as ghosts while our bodies stay here for everyone else to see. If we take our bodies everyone will follow and then it will no longer be our place.

(Tenet 4 from the Ghost Orchid manifesto:
We reveal only our likes and never our loves.)

Our violence gang protects our streets from the rival violence gangs (*the etceteras*), who surround us on all sides. They surround us but they can't beat us because they are weak against our super powers.

E. asks me if I want to play tennis today. I don't remember if my racquet still has strings. I used it in a street fight against injustice and I remember hearing the strings pop and snap with each strike! for justice.

Sometimes in the middle of our skirmishes I see E. lower her empty flower vase. I know she wants to go somewhere to become stranded. So do I but we're in a violence gang the likes of which the world has seen only a few times. If we go, others will follow.

I find my racquet and see that none of the strings are broken. I'm happy because E. and I can play. Tennis is fun.

5 x 4.6

Sunlight shines on our orange peels. It seems as if the gentle rays of sun-heat will burn them up. I'm worried that our apartment will catch fire. I go to the table and sweep the peels (now in the shape of a heart) into my hand and throw them out of the window. I think about them on the grass below. E. is not here. She left during the night. I heard her and wanted to tell her to stay. Instead, I stayed quiet.

It's good that she left in case we both burned up. It would be too late if, across the city somewhere, someone awoke to open a window to let the breeze in to cool the vestiges of a hot night, and saw the blood-red and orange conflagration creeping along the side of the old apartment building E. and I called home.

He or she would hesitate to make certain of what they were seeing and then, before calling for help, wake whoever was in bed still sleeping to come and look. But if that person who was in bed sleeping had also left in the middle of the night while the other person stayed quiet then it would be one person watching one other person overcome by fire.

x

~~logic alternatives~~

~~E. told me once that logic destroyed my way of thinking. But time is happening. This time and that time. Day and night. The lightness of day and the darkness of night. And the past may only represent the point at which all that happened to us starts to become vague memories or moments that we have forgotten. I told E. once that maybe time is a construct of memory. It was easier to tell her something I had no idea about than to tell her to stay.~~

~~I don't remember the future even though I've heard that it's already happened. I don't remember E. leaving and if she has already left tomorrow or next week or next year then I'm glad I don't remember. It's important that someone like me,~~

~~who wields a blood axe and walks the city perimeter ready to strike! for justice, forgets.~~

~~I quick cat to the kitchen, sidestep the refrigerator door that I opened, and grab the bottle of *suco de manga* that I save for when I am thirsty.~~

4

freedom waves

People by the sea look free. They sit in their sand freedom and play in their splashing water freedom. They lean back and give themselves to the sun freedom. They bask in the wind freedom. They run in the air freedom and fall onto the grass freedom. They exult in the outwardness of their bodies freedom.

But the waves will have their way and the people will want them more—the collision of temperatures, body vs. anti-body, the dopamine release of becoming free that is missing from being free.

The shoelace on one of my shoes has become untied but I don't have a moment to stop. I drift above the pavement that's stained by the blood of the unconvinced and the castaway chocolate sweets. The shoelace drags along the concrete and pops up and down as it collides with the pebbles on the thoroughfare and the detritus of unmindful pockets.

I think about the empty flower vase that is so empty but filled with so much power.

E. and I cuddle our life with our minds and our hearts. But we are like the detritus of unmindful pockets and the pebbles on the thoroughfare. We land where we are dropped and we go where we are kicked.

part J.

in the absence of an almighty

Kids try to be so muscular and cagey when they see adults because adults have unkind intentions and if a kid tries to be muscular and cagey then kind adults should understand because kind adults don't often trust each other. E. and I aren't kids but when we chop the word *chop* comes out of our mouths.

We're riding to the country again. We talk about chickens and planting radishes. There is room in our garden for radishes. All that is good comes from the sun and the rain. The rain is my translucent go. Sometimes it whispers and sometimes (in darkness) it shrieks. It whispers on your eyelashes and eyebrows. The sun is my opium den.

In the country store we hear someone playing a piano in the back room. I want to see the faces of those who sing their music and I want to see the hands of those who play it. We ring the bell.

He is a kid of the try-to-be-so muscular and cagey type. But E. hugs him and he is brave and (like all kids) he is beautiful. I ask him if he wants to join our violence gang. He says YES but only if he can bring his piano. We say YES. I tell him I wrote a darkness song but I have no music for it. I have words in my head but no music. I am not whole.

He tells us he wrote a book about a world where adults take care of kids. He tells us that we are his parents now. We promise to show him the parts of civilization that are good. He will be innocent until he is older and can no longer be innocent. And then he will become rebellious because he will want to be innocent again—what all rebels want to be but can never be again. He may even go on crime sprees with us and commit violence. For the sake of justice, I hope so.

6ix

stop stop hurry hurry

I have memories to forget and sometimes memories I think I have forgotten come back to me in images I can't piece together but that bring with them nausea. I feel grim (I am overcome and undone by grimness) but understand that a small erasing will erase the images and with it the feeling of nausea. But a piece of memory sometimes remains and even the smallest piece brings with it the same amount of nausea as the largest.

I am without my powers now. I am missing something. I must grow accustomed. My body is weary and fools me into thinking that my heart is weary too. But my heart is gone. Outside when the sun is shining, in my head it rains. Outside when it rains, in my head it rains harder. In my head I live in rain—in the rain of despair, in the rain of dread. The cloud water flows down my face and body, mixes with spit and sweat, and reaches the ground as blood. I decay in a world that decays and I am unmoved. I am truly one with the universe.

E. and I go to bed and through the window look for light in this night without end because this is a night of long waiting. The waiting for another day, for another succession of conversations and movements, for another morning of preparations to use up our energy that in a short time is replaced by weariness and the hindrance of sleep. But the night ends in time and the sun restores our ascension while darkness grieves in some other place. And though my heart is gone I still feel the missing aorta, the superior and inferior vena cava, the left and right ventricles, the atria.

I ask the flowers and grass and sky and sound of the river to give me more time. We know it to be true that with more time the heart moves to different places in the body. My heart was near my right shoulder when it disappeared. I think it pumped my blood into the ocean and followed my blood there. I want to go to the ocean. The ocean provides the salt that E. and I sprinkle onto the juicy avocado we eat with our spoon! of justice.

I am the bird. I am always here.

1

dandywarlions

I play a tambourine in our violence gang the Ghost Orchids. We play our music loud because our fans don't want to hear the grief in our lyrics. Back stage I read stories about children in wells or women disappearing in the Caribbean air or the excavation of the Babylonian war trench where undelivered letters and fragments of metacarpals are uncovered.

I'm in the hotel room waiting for you. I heard the news. Tell everyone I'll be there soon. But I can't move until you come and get me. The news is too sad. They found a letter from Margaret's dead husband that was never delivered and in it he wrote of his undying (but soon to be dead) love for her.

The enemy is brave...war...and should you get this letter...

This is love or maybe. I don't know. It's just another feeling. I can't ride the giant Ferris wheel that we watch from the park. I can only want to ride it and see you keep your hair away from your face when you're spinning on it. No one sits beside you and you're looking at me and smiling but I wonder if you're thinking that I'm frail.

All of the slow revolutions seem faster when I'm watching. Time moves faster for everyone. I'm always late or never there. I missed the war. I missed the downbeat in our song and the jingle from my tambourine never came.

But the song will play again and I promise to forget everything else and play my part on time. And the war will come again and I promise to write a letter in which I proclaim my undying love for you and reflect on how all of the savagery around me portends of a terminal impairment of the soft, human psyche.

~~I am here with drops of blood. Drops of blood and dark and tender meat. We can cook and let the aroma of our dinner waft. Waft out through the window and into the air of the public.~~

8twenty3

the ghost orchids get drenched

E. meets me in the hotel room. She's brought the violence gang with her. She sits with me and whispers that I am like a solitary, puffy cloud in the sky that means to bother the sun but is too kindly to bother and in any case the sun too mighty to be bothered.

We practice our new song: *stop stop hurry hurry*. Our practices are celebrations.

E. sings:

stop stop hurry hurry
you know my ways
are soft and furry
like a bunny rabbit
with a drinking habit
that's manageable
and keeps me in song
all day and all night
without any damage
that's outwardly visible

J. is on piano. A. is on drums. M. is on guitar. And I am on stage. E. moves between us as she sings. She hands me a tambourine and I jingle and I jangle. In between verses she looks over to me and tells me not to forget my shoulders.

55

9

[thursday]

I open the translucent envelope and look to its contents. But in those contents I see only the common renderings of a life that I know is complex and fraught with uncommon renderings. Too late did I realize that the envelope now drifting away from me in that eager wind that takes everything with it to sometimes unknown places, where sometimes I venture and sometimes not, were the real contents of your life, and that my chase of the envelope which will, according to the customs of the wind, become wet and afterwards too fragile to my touch to recover undamaged, will take me further away from you, during which time another reader, who understands the delicate nature and nuance of such envelopes, will read all that I should have read and seen all that I should have seen.

In the other life I am chasing and finding unknown places that capture my curiosity for brief moments and from which I must escape the disappointment of stumbling upon the meaningless.

In this life I think I've seen love as the following of a light that at night (alone) one fears. To near sleep and to think or dream that I have walked the streets at last light and mixed happily with all of the people of humanity gives me a feeling I can only describe as dread.

part 4 – letters to me from people who are both me and not me

1

for the daughters of Andromeda

Dear you an altogether faithless friend who is both me and not me,

If only the Ghost Orchids were around when men suppressed civilization, and so much so that the poets could not put their trust in this life and find the words to remind humans, animals, plants, and the gods themselves that they were all in grave danger.

Dear you an altogether faithless friend who is both me and not me,

If only the Ghost Orchids were around to do nothing but to live, to watch, to secretly write on the columns of those grand monuments to the small-minded and feckless men who honoured themselves in the marble and stone constructs (the decay of which we await at our peril) that last longer than the life of a single human being.

And yet here we are—our violence gang—one return away from making all right again in the way that life is both the cause and the effect of itself and then itself the cause and the effect of the living and so I say to both me and someone who is not me to be one of the living.

Love always,

Someone Who is Both Me and Not Me

8

the love-each-others

Dear Veil,

Yesterday I lay on the greenest and softest grass near the canna bush, taking in light and heat beneath the elephant ears that lilt in the breeze, the red and orange flowers of which stretched up to the sky and cast the shadows of their future blossoms onto my face and neck. I thought of the Ghost Orchids and a simple melody for them (the refrain *love love love*) while the curtain branches from the willow tree moved from side to side, as if opening and closing, to first reveal the house you once lived in, then two people holding hands and running to the beach, one of them throwing a bouquet of flowers into the air, then two people walking through the park under the *expansive paraplui*, then violence in the streets (the bottles, the bicycles, the shop windows), then the bustle of people on the Avenue of Children after the rain when the sun comes out again, then the sun by itself over a line of conifers, then the sun by itself over the ocean, then the sun by itself over the Ghost Orchids in the park who play the melody I created in my head, moving and happy. I wish you could hear it too.

Love,

Animal

2

TREE

Consider standing,

Of the trees I remember and will remember that in this life as in all other lives how I started my search (in the place and during the time in which I lived)—for another place and another time—at the bottom of some particular tree in the distance and then slowly looking up along its mighty (even if small) trunk until the land disappeared from my view and only the leaves and the sky behind them occupied the camera obscura of my plural oculus.

My gaze would linger there at the top of the tree where I would see the branches sway in the breeze until the feeling of freedom those branches conveyed became unbearable and my eyes moved slowly, as if falling in a more considerate gravity, down along the tree's mighty (even if small) trunk until the land reappeared but a different land.

I wondered on my way up where I would find myself when my eyes made their way back down but it was always the same place and the same time from where my journey began. Perhaps I fooled myself into being disappointed on my return but in spite of my quiet lament I knew that part of me was secretly relieved when I heard those familiar voices calling me back to where I belonged.

Standing still is gliding,

Pillipha

5

a real letter day

Dear JAME,

Today is a reminder of the day that all action began. The superpowers for ordinary people, the china song, the spider trap, the hut-hut-hut of moving barely an inch. Let's pummel and remember that when we pummel, we pummel with love. Let's cuff and remember that when we cuff, we cuff with love. So sleep tight until the morning when the music wakes you.

Yes, we must remember the music and the orchestra below our window—so finely in tune and harmonious with the breezes that converge from all parts of the world and flow by our little house. They bring molecules from other lands, from the atmosphere, and from the universe itself.

Our friend Saladin still appears here and there on my walk to clear his bearded throat and remind me of the unheard rumblings beneath the earth. The earth can seem flat even if it is bumpy. But underneath there are bumps that we try to smooth even though the smoothing does damage. You know that well. And it is a good thing to remember in our case so that underneath ourselves we don't mistake any other bone in our body for the heart bone. We will tap each other on that place on our body where our heart lies beneath as a reminder that it is okay to break all others but not this one.

When we last worked in the garden I saw a shed snake skin and buried it beneath the radish seeds. Also when drifting with famous anomalies such as driftwood observe the different pieces of wood that you can find from many different types of trees.

Love,

S?

12

rememory

Dear Queen of the Ghost Orchids,

I didn't think I would get this far. Simple words to speak to others is best. I feel like I am always telling you to remember this or that or asking you if you remember this or that. I think I am afraid that one day I will start to forget and I need someone to remember. But how is it possible to forget all of this? All of these feelings on the skin.

I hear it happens quite often. People are at war. They fight for justice (good or bad) and do great damage to others and themselves. I strike! for justice in my own way and have also done great damage—like those flowers I threw into the window glass. Do you remem—again (I smile with you).

I won't ask you to remember but please don't forget, which I suppose is almost the same, but perhaps makes you think that not forgetting is less tiresome than remembering. I'm trying to trick you my dear queen of the Ghost Orchids. My highest majesty of the Ghost Orchids. My Ghost Orchid queen of all present living and future living Ghost Orchids.

I want you to make a catalogue of the images. But only the good ones. If you can. And if you can't then together we'll build a machine that has a handle we can turn to chew up the *memoriam mala* of our never-long-enough lives together. A machine that chews up is a dangerous machine. But who in their darkest day in the darkest night would not confess to wanting a few turns?

Of course you will respond and then rightly say: but who in their greatest glory under the most magnificent sun on their brightest day would not also confess to wanting a few turns? I understand. I give you darkness and you give me light and I feel now that to occupy every part of the universe and to be one with humanity is to not exist as myself.

Maybe one day I will be able to bring the words up to the very top of my brain and remember back to you a new world that you don't remember but makes you feel the same as the old one. Choose me

in a long time the two of you to leave. I hear
Tuesday. But it is a day to choose. I hear that you
never lied. But only for you I don't regret that I
can't remember what day it is or who I am.

Amator Sors,

Endeavorus

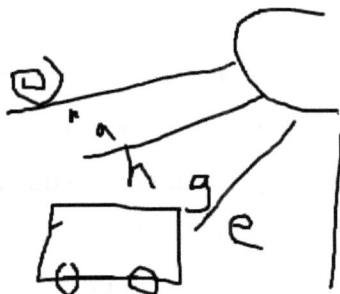

9

two people who live in a village walk through the town

Dear if-I-never-see,

Of sharp memory this can only be about. A memory that ignites and catches fire ever so briefly before being put out by the damper synapses of a pronounced but moist cerebral cortex. It may smoulder for a day but where once there was an electric connection there is now a wet rag flagging in the cold and heavy wind. In the village there are women and men who wear scarves and coats because in a village there is no difference between what is outside and what is inside. There are no buildings in the village but when the village becomes a town the new town people erect a building that comes to represent the women and men who live there.

It is from this building that people watch us when we walk through the town from our village. If we are holding hands and happy as we reach the

70

town we stop being happy and move our hands to our sides because happy people are punished in the town. But we know that one day we will rebel and bring happiness to the town. We give the people who watch us the briefest glimpse of this future in the way that our shoulders touch and how together we look up to the window from where they look down.

I think to myself that they want to take you because you are desirable to them but you will never go because to rebel is to live (honestly and fully) in a future that cannot become real until we are no longer here. It is ever so and we can live in no other way. ~~And when we are gone I know people from the village who will cry openly at our procession overcome by a collective grief. I know others who will cry privately away from the crowd on the shoulder of a lover or a friend or a stranger. And I know others still whose grief will be buried deep, who will go home alone, after all the tears of other mourners have been shed and when washing dishes or going up to the bedroom for the night, break down over the sink or collapse at the foot of~~

~~the stairs, and weep like they have never wept~~
~~before.~~

Etiam si omnes,

ego non

FOR

ALWAYS

I LOVE

YOU

uhmteenth imagined bird life

Dear Ms. or Mrs. Lovebird,

It says it is simple always in simple. The bird collects the feathers of other birds and lonely builds the ways of bird life other. E{m}ma+Lena Lovebird. Ms. or Mrs. Lovebird. Start with leaves and then continue. To left and tree side right and then to right and tree side left. Up in the pantomime of leaves near the fell of the lost lands of the mantis, go back to where the paths are unmarked. In this analogy *de la musica de la provincia*, the fermata hangs over the littlepaw mantis and the crowbelly monarch that face off among the red, yellow, and bearish leaves.

But who is this song I think? The love is remarkable. Was the heart even on before? The sun visits our village where we walk freely hand in hand to the horizon where, if I remember, it rains from the west. I can see how the rain corrosion is strong and undated carbon drips from the rotting fencewood to the ground where the grass is worn down to near dead. We can still place our hands there and think that we feel the earth. But everything we feel or think we feel or think we want to feel will be taken.

This way or the way of the crow? We see it up there by itself looking. Is it waiting for us to move or is it just a bird tired of flight? We are tired also. Tired enough of all this to get going. This way then. This way and this way only.

Love,
Mr. Lostbird

fray there the human bliss

dear e{m}ma+lena lovebird,

I see adventure in all of the loose strings that hang from the hem of your dress. The summer dress. The one you wear during all of your important travels. I hope you still wear it when the fall comes. Maybe you will wear it through winter also. And why not spring, which is only a short season away from the birthplace of such a dress? I know that not all of your travels to me are important but if I were to convince you that they were important or if you were to convince yourself that they were important then perhaps they might take on an importance.

But if not then let it be said and known to all that you have traveled to me in the past and implicit in your travel to me is the importance of the travel and that you and I were here under the sun during the summer and even when the clouds darkened the sky and the strange atmosphere, created by the layer of dust particles, that strangled the air beneath the clouds threatened our summer fun you did not leave my side.

And I feel that it is the same if you are wearing a different dress but some of the strings on your summer dress have come loose without me. I tell you that it is okay and I tell others that it is okay but deep down inside, which means not deep at all but just below the surface if there is even a surface, it is not okay. I want to make you a new dress if you will have it. I don't ask that you wear it. I don't know what I am asking. Maybe it will be the dress you wear for unimportant travels.

my arm is covered in skin and reaches out to you,

Mr. Lovelybird

5

the last letter before the start of the ending

Dear E+,

I don't remember my equation but that happens when you're living. You don't need to remember a thing when it becomes a part of you. I don't need to remember that I have arms and legs. But my equation came to me while other events were taking place. It's the equation for the happy/sad that we can't live without even when the right way of being happy brings itself and lets itself be known.

There are more anodyne explanations that describe the so-called understandings of what our lives might otherwise comprise but don't clarify for the spies. Live in disguise until you get home (the house you don't pass by) and can look or not look (the choice is yours) into loving eyes. The happy/sad is the vintage life.

It's like when we were sitting at the pub the name of which we didn't know because the letters on the outside window were faded and scratched up.

Me shirtless and you with that cigarette. You were talking about being a woman. So full of the goods you were and still are. We walked in on our way to somewhere else. I fixed my hair up so as to be presentable for the time being. The silver trinket on my neck chain rested on my breast plate. The one I won at the amusement park.

You asked me if I had the key. I took it from my pants pocket and held it up to show you. You told me to hold onto it. I nodded because I couldn't speak. Something was happening to me. I used the key to carve my equation into the bar wood: e{m}ma+. I don't forget it.

Love,

S?

2074

the note-like letter

Dear Panther Lily,

I want the Ghost Orchid music in my chest. I want it to replace my heart and other organs. Each note, each beat pushing through my skin here on this alien body. Sometimes softly so as not to appear violent and sometimes with great violence. As we, the great Ghost Orchids, greater even than our violence, march with our blood into the future.

But we can't keep the music from out there where everything we do is trapped in its vibrations and can only exist in between those always pulsating strings. All our words and gestures, even our most gentle, become transformed, and appear as performance in the spectacle of this new world.

We need a secret song—a secret piece of music—that we can keep to ourselves and take with us into the darkness and the silence, away from the spectacle, and let it do to us what it will and perhaps allow us to be our best selves for a moment that might seem longer than a moment but long enough to make us want to go on. You and I will always find a way. I wish you well as I have always wished you well. I love you as I have always loved you. I will not forget you.

For always,

Captain Tenderhooks

p.s. (wink)

SUPER POWERS FOR
ORDINARY PEOPLE

THE ORIGINS OF THE SUPERPOWERS
FOR ORDINARY PEOPLE

FIST OF STRONG

QUICK CAT

BLISTER BLOCK

TOE OF TERRIBLENESS

PINCH OF PECULIARITY

BRAIN THRUST

FEATHER FINGER

KNEE OF KNOCKING (*ORIGIN UNKNOWN*)

ELBOW OF INVINCIBILITY (*ORIGIN UNKNOWN*)

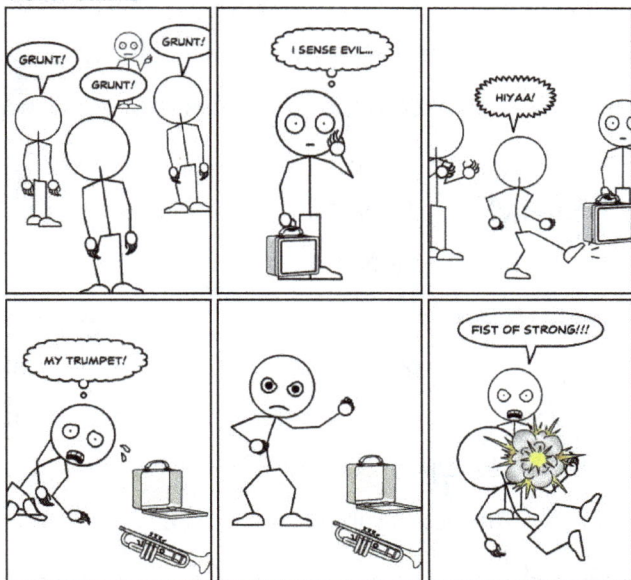

the fist of STRONG (or EVIL IN THE ALLEY)

The first time I used the 'fist of strong' I trembled. It was so powerful it made me sick. I was on my way back from a trumpet lesson (trumpet = the most beautiful sculpture in the world) and I got cornered in an alley. Alleys still exist today—pathways without exits, doors on either side closed. I was lost. It was dark and the darkness around me searched for more darkness. I didn't notice the boys following me. They seemed to come from nowhere and blocked my escape. They made fun of my shoes (yes, there was a time when boys made fun of shoes!). Then they moved in close. They didn't speak unless you call grunting speaking. Not all of them were evil but I sensed EVIL in one of them. I had sensed treachery before but never evil. And I was right because the evil ONE kicked my trumpet case out of my hand. The case popped open when it hit the ground and my trumpet tumbled out. The other boys snickered. They weren't evil but they couldn't recognize evil WHICH is almost as bad. I became angrier than I had ever been in my life. I snapped and unleashed the most powerful punch I had ever unleashed. I think that I might have become evil too—for a split second. I yelled out "FIST OF STRONG!" and knuckle-sandwiched the boy's chest sending him flying back (all the way back) into the dead end of the alley. I left my arm outstretched, my fist still in the air, and turned my eyes toward the other boys. They ran away which turned out to be a good thing because I started trembling from the amount of power I had unleashed.

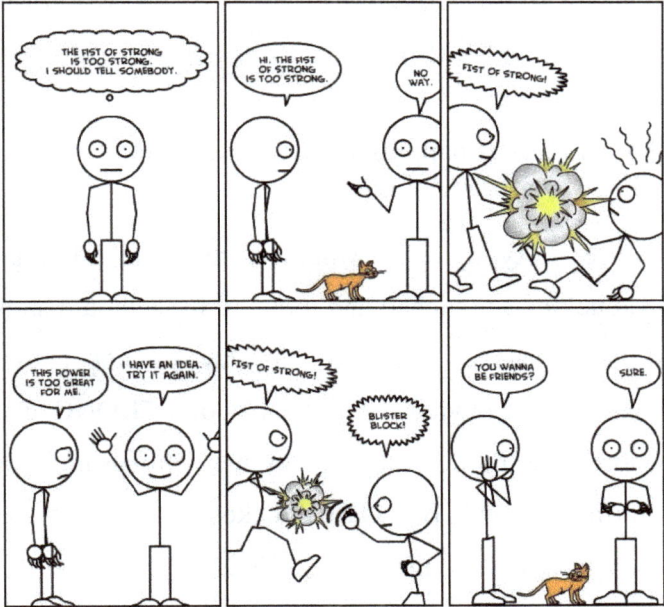

the BLISTER block!

I was minding my own business when I heard two…whatever they are…talking and then one…whatever they are…knuckle-sandwiched the other…whatever they are…with a fist of STRONG and then afterwards looked sad—sadder than the…whatever they are…that got knuckle-sandwiched. Who knew that…whatever they

87

are…could be filled with such regrets like I am sometimes filled with?

It's a strange happy/sad world we live in.

I felt pity for the…whatever they are…that got knuckle-sandwiched and thought that I should show the…whatever they are…a way of not getting knuckle-sandwiched by the fist of STRONG ever again but the…whatever they are…thrust(hint!) his arm out and BLISTER-blocked the soon-to-be-arriving-to-the-chin fist of STRONG!

(I was speakless.)

I knew I had to join forces with the…whatever they are…and learn their ways. I also knew that I had ways that I could teach them because I could sort of tell they didn't know what they were doing.

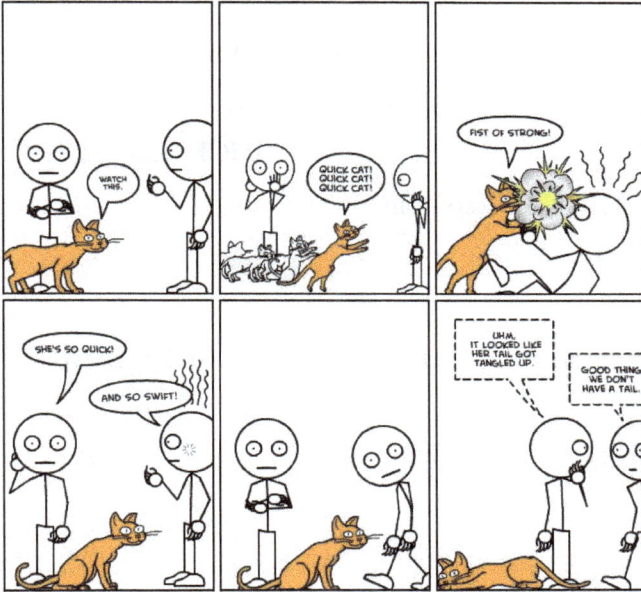

'QUICK CAT'

QUICK cat

Now that we had joined forces we practiced the QUICK cat in slow motion until we perfected it. We gave each other fist-bumps of success (not a real superpower but just a way of celebrating). We added the FIST OF STRONG move to the QUICK cat to create the QUICK cat/FIST OF STRONG combination move. We practiced on each other and tried to BLISTER-block the FIST OF STRONG like we normally would but we were too slow because the QUICK cat made it impossible to see the blow coming. The QUICK cat/FIST OF STRONG combination move is virtually unstoppable.

Combination 1: QUICK cat/FIST OF STRONG

Quick cat! Quick cat! Quick cat! FIST OF STRONG!!!

Pummeling soon follows.

Toe of Terribleness

Lazy days…la-zy days. It was the perfect day. Friday and a snow day. A day to practice the superpowers for ordinary people and just drink some chocolate milk afterwards. I was lying down on the couch underneath a warm blanket, except for my big toe, which stuck out like a sore thumb. My thumb was warm like a big toe underneath a warm blanket should be. But my friend was practicing the QUICK cat (he wanted to be even quicker) and then surprised me by trying to hit me with a FIST of STRONG. I was helpless. Or so I thought. I instinctively stuck out my foot and my toe made devastating contact with his knuckles. He grabbed his hand and while he was doing that I bombarded him with toe strikes from both my right and left foot. The strikes were so devastating I became lost in my own power until I saw my friend collapse on the ground. I was happy that I found a new superpower for ordinary people but I realized that these kinds of superpowers can really go to your head. When it comes to superpowers it seems like half of learning how to use them is to control how super they are. I wasn't sure if we should share them with the world because there are a lot of people who might use these super powers for evil and not for good. I felt bad about unleashing the toe of terribleness on my friend and made some chocolate milk for him while he was recovering on the floor. I wanted some also.

Pinch of Peculiarity

Stefan?

Why the yellow umbrella and not the red one today? It's because of what happened the night before when we were walking home from the bookstore. We bought a book about sharks. The rain was loud and you tried to call me but I couldn't hear you because the rain was hitting the ground and the buildings and the cars like nails and making that crescendo sound that stays at crescendo all the time. I was thinking *What would happen if I gave you a fist of strong right to your jaw? In the rain.* There would be a huge splash if we were near a puddle. I might laugh but I don't think you would laugh. I only do things if the chances are good that we'll both laugh. If I was sure that I was going to laugh and you might laugh then I would do something. If you didn't laugh I could still convince you that it was funny. You still might not laugh but you would understand. Then I started thinking about hedgehogs and two hermit crabs. But I couldn't hear you calling me and instead of yelling to get my attention you pinched me on my arm and I went flying into a huge puddle and thinking *What was that?!.* I thought that pinch was peculiar. I was completely wet and my red umbrella smashed sideways into the sidewalk and broke but I was also excited because we had discovered another super power for ordinary people. It looked like a great white shark was swimming in the puddle because the book about sharks fell out of my bag and landed with the front cover facing up.

For a split second I was afraid of putting my hand in the puddle and getting the book. I reached into the puddle but had my hand in the PINCH of PECULIARITY position ready just in case. But I got the book and nothing happened. We had to walk home underneath your umbrella. I wanted the part of my arm where you pinched me to be in the rain though to absorb all the healing powers of the water. The pinch of peculiarity wrecked my arm. But that's why I'm using the yellow umbrella today. It's still raining after raining all day yesterday. I wish I could use the pinch of peculiarity on the clouds.

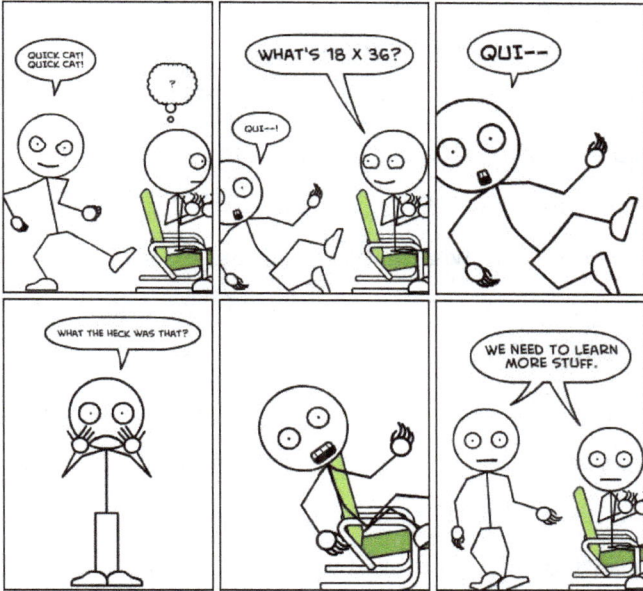

the BRAIN thrust!

Of all the devastating superpowers for ordinary
people the BRAIN thrust is probably the second
most difficult to master. I don't know if that's true
but I have never been able to do the most powerful
superpower for ordinary people (hint!). The BRAIN
thrust looks like it's just used for defense but it can
quickly change the outcome of a situation by

stunning your opponent. I was practicing my superpowers for ordinary people while my friend was doing his homework. I was finished with my homework. I was actually in the middle of practicing the QUICK cat/FIST OF STRONG combination when my friend asked me what the answer to 18 x 36 was because he ran out of room on his paper to work out the multiplication. I completely stopped my move. Or I was stopped in the middle of my move—somewhere in the middle of the QUICK cat—because my BRAIN was thrusted. He could have used any superpower on me while my BRAIN was thrusted because I was completely helpless.

But then we noticed something strange. Since he didn't know the answer to his own question, his move (just sitting there doing his homework) was stopped in the middle because he apparently thrusted his own BRAIN by not knowing the answer to the question he asked me. So we experimented with the BRAIN thrust and figured out that if you use the BRAIN thrust you have to know the answer to the question that you're asking or you end up thrusting your own BRAIN. If your opponent knows the answer to the question you're asking then you also end up thrusting your own BRAIN. So we decided to start learning more things at school just in case. And not just in school. We decided to learn more things all the time.

Feather Finger

There is only one human being in the world who has mastered the greatest super power for ordinary people: the feather finger. And it's not me. I have tried to practice the feather finger but I have never been able to do it. I read in some ancient text that the feather finger can't be practiced. It can only be done. I think it's the only super power for ordinary people that we didn't invent. We read about it in the ancient texts. I don't know if those are ancient rumors or if my friend wrote the ancient texts to make sure no one else practices the feather finger so that one day they'll also be able to do it. I still practice it but I have never been able to do it. Sometimes my friend and I are battling and I think I have the advantage with a QUICK cat/FIST OF STRONG/PINCH of PECULIARITY combination but then the feather finger knocks me out. I can't even feel it. That's why it's called the feather finger. My friend says he usually just touches me on my nose and says "feather FINGER" but I never feel it or hear it and then I'm defeated. There's no defense for the feather finger (not even the blister block!) but the feather finger can't be used all the time. Apparently my friend never knows if it's going to work so it's risky. But so far it's always worked for him. So lucky. I tried to do it over and over and over again one time when we were battling but it never worked for me so I got really pummeled.

"Feather finger!"

"Elbow of invincibility!"

"Aye! Feather finger!"

"Knee of knocking!"

"Aaaaaah! Feather finger!"

"Pinch of peculiarity!"

"Mother fu! Fea-ther fing—"

And then I don't remember much after that except that we were drinking hot chocolate and talking about how I shouldn't curse and also that I probably shouldn't try that again. I'm going to keep practicing though. The one thing the super powers for ordinary people teaches people is to never give up and keep practicing even if the ancient texts say otherwise.

Keep battling!

www.ingramcontent.com/pod-product-compliance
Lightning Source LLC
Chambersburg PA
CBHW072040040426
42447CB00012BB/2951